The Road to Tangible Hope

AN ETHIOPIAN WOMAN'S
TALE OF SURVIVAL,
STRENGTH, AND INSPIRATION

To my Dear Friend
Diane

What People Are Saying About
The Road to Tangible Hope

"Lily Yoseph puts the lie to 'there's nothing we can do.' Beginning by finding sponsors for poor girls from her native Ethiopia, she has assembled a cracker-jack team, now serving 140 girls, who are dedicated not only to their learning, but their safety. She's a force of nature. The shape of compassion itself. Read this story and be prepared to be moved."
—Peter Coyote | Zen Buddhist priest, author and actor

"*The Road to Tangible Hope* chronicles the remarkable life of author Lily Yoseph: a moving tale of one woman's indomitable determination to survive amidst some of the darkest hues of the human experience."
—James Redford | filmmaker, environmentalist
Note from the author: Sadly, James Redford had passed prior to this printing. He was actively encouraging me to share my story and I will forever remember his warm and thoughtful support.

"Lily Yoseph's book is a powerful testament to the indomitable human spirit and the strength that lies within each of us to overcome adversity. It serves as a reminder that even in the darkest of times, there is always a glimmer of hope.

"Moreover, Lily's commitment to helping young girls in Ethiopia is nothing short of inspiring. Her selfless efforts to uplift and empower others demonstrate the profound impact that one person can make in the lives of many. Through her initiatives, she is creating real change, providing hope, and opening doors to a brighter future for these girls. I wholeheartedly recommend this book to anyone seeking inspiration, courage, and a reminder of the boundless possibilities that exist when we find our own way."
—Lisa Kristine | Humanitarian Photographer

The Road to Tangible Hope

AN ETHIOPIAN WOMAN'S
TALE OF SURVIVAL,
STRENGTH AND INSPIRATION

Telile Yoseph

Adu Publishing
Sausalito, California

Adu Publishing
1001 Bridgeway Ste. A-1
Sausalito, CA 94965
tangiblehope.org

NOTE Some names have been changed to protect the privacy of individuals mentioned in this book.

Ordering Information:
Quantity sales. Special discounts are available on quantity purchases by corporations, associations, and others. For details, contact the "Special Sales Department" at the address above.

The Road to Tangible Hope: An Ethiopian Woman's Tale of Survival, Strength, and Inspiration / Telile Yoseph. -- 1st ed.
ISBN 979-8-9892624-0-3 paperback
ISBN 979-8-9892624-1-0 ebook
ISBN 979-8-9892624-2-7 audiobook

This book is dedicated to
my loving father and uncle
and my two wonderful mothers.

Contents

Introduction

I met Telile Yoseph, nicknamed Lily, about ten years ago when I attended an inspiring presentation she gave about the work she was doing with young girls in Ethiopia. She first showed us pictures of sick, under-nourished, sad little girls. Then, we saw pictures of the same girls after she provided them with health care, nutrition, education, and personal mentoring. In the second set of pictures, the girls were glowing with health and confidence. I was sitting there with tears running down my face. I had to help. Soon, Lily and I became close collaborators on this mission. Since Lily spoke four languages – two Ethiopian languages, Dutch and English – I became the native English speaker who put Lily's thoughts on paper.

So it was that Lily told me she had amazing stories from her life that she had told no one. Even people close to her did not know the heart-wrenching, life-threatening experiences she had endured. My husband Floyd and I decided to rent a cottage on Vancouver Island, Canada and take Lily there so I could record her life story.

Every morning, Lily would cook breakfast for Floyd and me and then he would take off for the day, leaving Lily and me to work on her story. Lily would lay on the floor, her story unfolding in her lovely, low, melodious voice. I would sit on the couch with my computer on my lap recording this amazing, twisted tale of her incredible strength, survival, and, especially, her spirit. Please note that this manuscript is short but dense and intense and it is written in direct, short sentences in the cadence of Lily's speech when she speaks in English. In a way, you are hearing Lily speak. This is Lily's story.

Janet Dean, Tangible Hope Foundation Board Member

Grandmother Ako

My grandmother Ako had 18 children with one man. There were three sets of twins. She was a midwife and delivered my family's babies. She was a very strong, bold, and a beautiful woman. She was tall and carried herself with confidence. She had a bright smile with beautiful straight white teeth. She was well-known as a psychic and a healer who had incredible charisma. People were drawn to her. They would line up in front of her house, waiting for the medicines that she would concoct for their various illnesses. My family said I was just like my grandmother. I even inherited a dark streak along the side of my tongue (it's called the snake tongue). That, in my culture means that when you curse someone, it sticks.

Before I was born, Ako worked for wealthy people doing small jobs to earn enough money to send her children to school. She was illiterate but wanted her children to have an education. She managed to educate nearly all 18 of her children, and most of them did well in life.

Grandmother in her garden

Ako and her husband, my grandfather, lived as a loving couple for many years. Sadly, he died of pneumonia when I was about three years old. She mourned him so deeply that the sadness never really left her eyes.

By the time of my grandfather's death, Ako had earned enough money to have beehives, cows, sheep, chickens, and a huge vegetable and flower garden. On honey harvest day, we children were given the raw honey-combs as a treat. The sticky sweet syrup dripped down our chins as we happily slurped it up. Everything was delicious at grandmother's house. She made a traditional Ethiopian dish, called *inset,* from shredded roots that were buried in the earth for three months. It is very healthy and high in mineral content. Every time I smell it and taste it, I can see my grandmother standing tall and smiling at me. She was the matriarch of the family, and everyone loved her, listened to her advice, and respected her decisions.

Childhood

I was an only child. My mom and dad met each other at the Swedish missionary school in Kofele, Ethiopia. My dad was raised in the Swedish missionary orphanage there, because when he was 13 years old, his mother and father died within one month of each other. We think they died of pneumonia, but there is no way of knowing for sure.

My father, Yoseph, was the oldest of four boys. Of course, I never got to meet his parents (my paternal grandparents). My father told me they had a huge farm with cattle, horses, sheep, and chickens. When my father's parents died, my dad's uncle took all the wealth and property for himself. The family thought he would take the four boys, too. However, he did not want them and did not take care of them. My father, all alone with one of his younger brothers, walked many miles to the Swedish Missionary to ask if they would take them in. The kind missionaries gave him and his younger brother food, a place to sleep, school clothes, and enrolled them in school. Soon, my father went back to get his other two brothers so they could go to school there, too. The third brother was also taken in by the missionaries. One brother, who was too young for school remained with his uncle. He worked on the farm over the years and later became a farmer himself. My father understood how important this opportunity to go to school was and studied very hard so he would do well. Later, he became a teacher at the missionary school that he had attended. That's where he met my mother who was also a student at the missionary school and became a teacher there as well.

They fell in love and were married. One year later, I was born. I was a fat little girl, so my grandmother called me Gonjoba, the little chubby one. I was baptized in the Swedish Missionary Church. My baptismal name was Mehreat. It's a biblical name meaning forgiveness. It was prescient, as I would have much need for forgiveness in my life.

When I was old enough, I started going to Sunday school. My friends were the Swedish kids in kindergarten. I had a handsome blue-eyed blond friend named Adam. I was completely obsessed with him. I loved that he was so different from Ethiopian kids. We became great friends, and I often played with him and his sister.

My father played piano in Sunday services. Every Sunday I looked forward to going to church to listen to dad's music and especially, to see my crush, Adam. We spent a couple of years attending school and church together. I told my father, "When I grow up, I'm going to marry Adam." Father answered, "We'll see."

My birthmother, me, age 4, my dad

While I was still in kindergarten, I visited my father's classroom. The world map was hanging on the wall. I told my dad, "Daddy, I want to go here, here, and here," pointing to different places on the map. "I want to meet people from all around the world." My dad assured me,

"You will see the world and meet many people. First, you must finish school."

My father will always be my hero. He helped me believe that it would be possible to do whatever I wanted to do in my life. And that, eventually, I would explore the world. Especially, he gave me the self-confidence and permission that I could do anything. It was so culturally unique for him, an Ethiopian man, to have this open attitude towards his daughter. Most Ethiopian girls did not have a dad like mine, and they were regularly punished for being disobedient or thinking independently. The girls I knew were jealous of me and they told me that they wished they had my dad instead of their mean ones. My father never punished me. Instead, if I did something wrong, he sat me down like an adult and explained how what I had done hurt him and why. He gave me so much love that I never wanted to disappoint him.

Although it was happy, life was pretty busy and hectic at my house growing up. My parents took in children who lived too far from the school to attend. They would give them food and lodging, and the kids would go home on weekends. So, we always had a houseful of stray kids. I was pretty jealous when the other kids got my parents' attention. But the example of their generosity has stayed with me.

My dad built a couple of houses on our land with the help of the missionaries. Our home was outside of the Swedish compound but nearby. Our land was lush with many beautiful trees and flowers. My dad rented out the two extra houses we had on the property to Americans who were in the Peace Corps.

I became friends with two Peace Corps ladies from Washington, DC. They baked wonderful cookies and shared them with me whenever I visited. One of them asked my dad if she could adopt me and take me to America. My dad refused and told her that when I reached the age of 18, she could invite me to go to school in the US. She sent me clothes and toys every Christmas for many years. I never got that invitation, though. I remain disappointed when people do not keep their promises…which is often.

Mom

When I was five years old, my mom was making injera (Ethiopian food) with her sister. She finished all the cooking and cleaning and went to take a shower. In those days, the shower was a concrete room where you brought a bucket of warm water to wash yourself. The water was too hot, so her sister went back to the kitchen to bring more cold water. When she got back, mom had fallen on the floor. When mom's sister saw her laying there, not moving, she screamed. Everyone rushed into the shower to try to help, but they were unable to rouse her. They covered mom's naked body with a white cloth and called the missionary doctor. Two doctors came to try to revive mom, but it was too late. She was gone. We don't really know what happened since there was no medical inquiry at that time.

My memories of my mother's death are through the eyes of a confused child.

My birth mother, Robdu

At the time mom died, I had been playing with the neighbor's kids. When I came home, I could see the sadness in my dad's face. I had never seen my father cry before. I didn't know what had happened or what it meant to be dead. My grandmother was screaming. It was total chaos. I could see people screaming, moaning, and beating themselves. Word traveled fast in our village, and it wasn't long before our house was filled with mourners. In our culture, when a loved one dies, they express their grief openly and loudly. They beat their chest and shake their heads and wail and keen. I had never seen this before and did not understand all this dramatic commotion. I only cried because my dad was crying and then more people found out and more people came into our house as the screaming and moaning continued late into the dark night. The following morning, the house finally quiet, the family got together and began to plan my mother's funeral.

My mother was much loved. On the day of the funeral, people came from all over Ethiopia. Now, there was a great crowd of perhaps one hundred people or more beating their chests and wailing. As a child, I was simply mesmerized by the spectacle. I watched them with wide, unknowing eyes.

That day my uncle, my mother's brother who loved her very much, came to the graveyard where they were to bury my mom. No one had told him who had died. They had just told him to come to a funeral. When he learned that it was his sister, my mother, who had died, he collapsed onto the ground and sobbed uncontrollably.

My mom's body was carefully dressed and put into a coffin to be carried to the graveyard. People marched alongside, mourning loudly. I was holding my dad's hand and watched as they lowered the box into the ground and three men covered the box with dirt. When we went back to the house, there was a huge tent set up outside and piles of traditional Ethiopian food were being served. I still didn't realize my mom was gone. It just didn't register in my little girl's mind. In the evening, we went back into our house and slept. I was just an exhausted little girl.

Since mom was not there, the days and weeks that followed felt strange. Everyone was hugging me and kissing me and consoling me because I had just lost my mother. My mother's sister, my auntie Adie, was still with us, though. I knew her well because she had helped take care of me since birth. Having her close made me feel that everything would be all right. She stayed with us and took care of my dad and me. We had a maid to cook for us, but auntie was always there helping and loving me. Life was okay.

My New Mom

After a couple of months, my grandmother, Ako, along with the local elders decided that I should not have to grow up with a stepmother. They decided that my auntie would marry my father and become my mother and his wife. All this was decided for Auntie, and she had no say in the matter. It was sad for her but good for me.

My grandmother and a couple of uncles took my auntie to a different town until everything was settled. They basically kidnapped her even though her brothers did not agree to the match. Auntie was forced by my grandmother, the matriarch of the family who had absolute authority, to marry my father. This was so that I would be raised by a woman who loved me and was part of the family.

Having Auntie Adie living with us made me very happy. She was like my mom. In Oromo tradition, it is not unusual to marry the sister after the wife dies. My auntie, my mom, is the best thing that ever happened to me. She had always loved me. However, her love for me became even stronger after my mom died. Over the years, I came to realize how special she was and what a huge sacrifice she had made for me. There is no way I could ever repay her for giving up her own future life to marry my father and raise me with such loving kindness and patience. She had taken care of me since I was born, and now she was my real mother.

Me and my auntie/mom in Portland

Her example of kindness has always inspired me. She sacrificed her life to raise me. She adopted kids off the street so they could go to school. She was always generous. Before she put any food in her mouth, she fed us.

One day, while sitting with my father, I asked, "Will my mom ever come back again?" Dad told me, "She is in heaven now. One day we are all going to join her." I asked, "What does heaven look like?" Dad explained, "It is beautiful and green. There is all the food you could ever want and everything you need is provided. It is a very happy place." But I still saw sadness in my dad's eyes and asked him if he was okay. He always told me, "All is well."

After my dad and auntie were married, I was still an only child. I often asked my dad if I was ever going to have sisters and brothers like the other kids. My dad assured me that one day I would have a lot of brothers and sisters.

Life went on and soon, my auntie/mom got pregnant. I was so excited that I was going to have a little brother or sister. My dad got a promotion, and we moved to another city. We rented our house to the American Peace Corps and left Kofele. My new mom's due date came, and she went into labor in the city of Karsa's Swedish missionary clinic. Her labor lasted 24 hours. It was a very difficult labor, and she almost died because the baby was so big. She was lucky that the doctor who delivered the baby had just come from Sweden and knew how to deliver such a big baby.

I was so excited to see my new sister that I couldn't sleep all night. When I saw her for the first time, no one could separate us. After all this time alone, I finally had a sister!

After a couple of years, we went back to Kofele, and Mom got pregnant with her second child. Mom's second pregnancy was difficult. She was nauseated for nine months. When labor finally came, my grandmother was the midwife and delivered my second sister. The delivery went smoothly this time. My new sister Arfasa was beautiful with amazing thick black hair. My prayers were answered. I had two sisters. After going to school, I rushed home to see my sisters. Then, I started asking for a brother. One year later, mom got pregnant again. I was happily expecting a brother. Indeed, my brother Orma was born. My dad was so happy he shot his gun into the air in celebration. Eventually, I was one of seven siblings.

School

Because I was a tomboy, most of my friends in school were boys. I still have better relationships with some of my men friends than with women. When I was 15, I was involved in a lot of sports. In soccer, I was the fastest runner on the team, a skinny girl with short hair who ran like a train. They used to yell, "Is #7 a girl or a boy?" I participated in gymnastics, volleyball and I ran the 200-meter event for my school track team. One semester we had to compete with a different school. I went on the big bus with the whole team to the town of Assela about 99 miles away from Kofele.

Our team coach was also our gymnastics teacher and a classroom teacher. His name was Berket. He gave me the creeps because I could always feel his hungry eyes on me. He kept trying to get me to come to his house and was always flirting with me. I was constantly side-stepping his advances because I knew that if I was ever alone with him, he would rape me as he had other girls at my school. I always refused his invitations, so I became a challenge for him. He was known to be a "womanizer" and had been successful in intimidating and coercing every girl he wanted except me.

I was determined to stand up to him, to be bold, and not allow myself to be intimidated. We arrived at the Assela high school where we all stayed in the same hotel, including our coach. The first day of the competition, I injured my ankle while I was running but I still came in at third place. After my team finished the competition and received their prizes, they returned to the bus to go home to Kofele. I had decided to stay a couple more days to visit with family who lived in Assela.

My coach was very angry that I had made this decision without his knowledge. However, I had already received permission to stay from my father.

A few days later, when I returned to school in Kofele, I was taking a class from the coach. I was filling out a quiz, and he came up to my desk and wrote a big C on my paper. I was shocked because I always got A's. I shouted, "This is not correct!" He told me in front of everyone to get out of his class and followed me to the door to intimidate me. My rage escaped. I had a big ringed binder in my hands and crashed the edge of it deep into his neck. Next, I punched him hard in the stomach, lunged and bit him deep in the chest, drawing blood, which I could taste. Finally, I soccer kicked him in the groin, and he buckled to the floor.

Teachers from all the classes came out to separate us. I was screaming at him, "You are not going to get away with this! I am going to expose what you have done to me and to many girls. I am going to tell the world!" Another teacher came and took me to the principal's office. I told him what he had tried to do to me and what he had done to many other girls in the school.

I was taken to Kebele, the detention office, to be disciplined. I was locked into a room and had to sit on a hard bench. A guard stood outside the door. Even as a child, you must stay there day and night until you are released. While I was there, one of my good friends, Emu, was detained as well. At least I had company.

While I was in detention, my father was serving the country. He was mayor of Kofele and had gone to negotiate with guerilla fighters in Baila province in an attempt to bring peace. He would ride his horse back and forth between the two sides, carrying messages in an attempt to convince both sides not to fight. The governor had chosen my dad to do this because the guerilla fighters were of my dad's tribe, Oromo. Oromo are the majority tribe in Ethiopia. The people who were appointed by the government were Amhara, and they were always suspicious that my dad would side with the Oromo guerillas because they were of the same tribe. But my dad always stood for peace and believed in bringing all the tribes together.

After I spent the second day in detention, that night, around 8 pm, the guard knocked on the door. I was sitting with my friend, Emu. He said, "Officials want to question you. Would you come with me?" I had no choice, so I agreed to go with him, but I felt a chill pass through my body. While we were walking, I asked him where we were going. He told me we were going back to the high school where I had a fight with my teacher. When we arrived at the high school, I was taken to a room where all the district leaders solemnly greeted me. I knew most of them through my father. They started asking me questions about my dad. They asked me if he was an Oromo liberation front member. That question was completely unexpected since I was in trouble for fighting with a teacher.

Every question they asked I answered with a loud and clear "I don't know"! They sat me on the floor, held me down and the torture began as one big man started hitting me hard on the feet with a heavy rope. He kept hitting my feet, and I kept answering, "I don't know!" until my feet became numb and started to swell. Since they didn't learn anything from me, they finally gave up and had the guard take me back to the detention center.

The next morning, I was in agony, could not walk and my feet were weeping. My mom brought breakfast, and I told her what had happened to me. She called my dad who quickly returned from his duties. Dad called the district government and complained about his daughter being tortured while he was trying to bring peace. I was called in to the district attorney's office in Assela for questioning. I told him what had happened to me while in detention and also about how so many girls had suffered sexual mistreatment by this teacher that I had attacked, but they were too afraid of him to talk about it.

This district attorney knew my uncle and wanted to help. So, he got the head of the police department involved, who ordered an investigation. All the city council members were then put in jail for torturing me. And the teacher, Berket, was also arrested. Everyone in town learned about it and the girls who this teacher had abused became emboldened and told their stories. He had even gotten one girl pregnant.

I was very happy that justice would be done, and my father was relieved that I was now safe from this predator at school. After gathering all the evidence, they all had to appear in court. They were sentenced for from one to three years. The teacher who had attempted to sexually abuse me lost his license to teach and got three years in prison. He never returned to Kofele. Even as a young girl, I fought to defend myself and bring truth into the light. For some reason, I was both fearless and fierce. I cursed them and it stuck!

Kuyera

I was in middle school, and it was summer vacation. I decided it would be fun to go visit my girlfriend Dureti who lived about 30 miles from Kofele. When Dureti's mother came to pick me up, I was looking forward to my vacation. The plan was to spend two months of the summer there with Dureti and her family.

While I was in Kuyera, I met Robel, a nice young man who was studying at the Seventh Day Adventist College. In the summer, he drove Dureti's family's mini-bus between Kuyera and Shashamane. I had a favorite bakery in Shashamane, so I asked Robel to pick up some cake for us on his way home. He was so kind and gentle that whatever we asked for he would bring to us. He would become a lifelong friend.

In the summer evenings, we would all gather around a big bonfire to eat. We had many lively, playful conversations. We teased and made fun of each other, and I continued to express my bold, independent opinions. It became a ritual, and we all looked forward to gathering in the evening to talk and laugh. It was a wonderful summer vacation away from school until one day, it wasn't.

Dureti's mother began talking to us about a special procedure. But she never really told us what it was. She explained that it was so important for a girl to have it done in order to be a "good girl." I was young and naïve, and I trusted her. So, I told Dureti's mother, "I want to be a good girl." She was so happy. She did this without consulting with my family. Without any idea of what this commitment meant, I agreed to be a "good girl."

One evening, we all gathered around the fire. We roasted fresh corn and were eating, laughing, and talking. Dureti's mother was there. She started talking about what makes a woman pure. All Dureti's family was there except her father. He had gone to Addis Ababa to bring medicine for his pharmacy.

Dureti's mother said, "It's time." She meant that it was time for Dureti and me to go through "The Procedure." I don't remember what she really called it at the time. "We should do it on this summer break," she said, convincingly. I had no idea what this really meant. I was so brain-washed about being a "good girl."

Being a good and brave girl, I agreed to go through with it. Dureti's mother arranged for a local lady who was experienced at "cutting." We set the date. I had no fear and was willing to go through it without my parent's permission. Dureti's father was gone as well. So, it was perfect timing for her to do this without any interference from our families.

One member of Dureti's family set up a "quiet room." They put a mattress on the floor. They put a plastic tarp on the mattress and prepared a sharp blade. They also brought in two men and a rope to tie us down.

They started the cutting. Dureti was first. I was outside. She went through it. I was waiting to hear her scream…but she didn't. Somehow, I didn't hear a noise from her. I didn't know that they had stuffed a blanket in her mouth. I thought to myself that it would be okay.

I was next. My new friend, Robel, and all Dureti's siblings were waiting outside. I entered the room and quickly became filled with dread. Two big men lowered me to the mattress and held me down. They forcefully spread my young legs.

I was completely vulnerable in front of these strong, scary men. I knew I had made a big mistake, but I realized that I had given away my power and there was no going back. I was physically trapped. The lady held the blade and without any anesthesia started to try to cut off my clitoris. I was screaming like crazy and squirming to try to avoid her cuts. I felt a white fire course through my whole body and clear out the top of my head. I screamed until I had no voice left and all that came out was a hoarse bellow.

The process did not go well. My blood started streaming down on the plastic tarp like a river. It was shooting out with every beat of my heart. The lady who cut me and Dureti's mother were terrified, dropped to their knees and were loudly praying to god to stop the bleeding. I was still confused about what had really happened. But when I saw Dureti's mother crying and praying, I realized I was really in danger.

They finally called a nurse. When she got there, I told her, "Oh my God, I can't explain what I just went through." No one in my family knew. They thought I was having a great time with my friend and her family for the summer, but it was hell. Eventually, the nurse was able to stop the bleeding, and, because of my struggling, the cutting was not completely "successful." That very important part of my body was still intact.

The next day, when I had to pee it burned like fire. Dureti had it easy. It hurt, but not as bad as it hurt me, and she had hardly bled.

Dureti's father returned from Addis Ababa. When he found out that we had been mutilated, he was furious. He told Dureti's mother that what she had done to us was incredibly cruel. He vowed that none of his other daughters would ever be cut.

Dureti's mother slaughtered a sheep to feed us. I had lost a lot of blood and needed nourishment to recover. She made sure I had a meal at least four times a day, plus snacks. Gradually, I started to feel better.

Dureti's mother felt so guilty after her husband told her how cruel it was for her to perform cutting on her own, and on someone else's child, that she tried to make it up to me. She gave me anything I wanted. I knew she still loved me and always would. I didn't really blame her, and I wasn't feeling angry. Like so many others in third world countries where they practice FGM (Female Genital Mutilation), she was just ignorant. This was all she knew. In her world, in order to be a "good girl" you must sacrifice sexual pleasure. It had happened to her, and she gave us the same. This cutting is illegal in Ethiopia now, but it still happens.

After the two-month vacation was over, I went back to my family. I told the story of what had happened to my father and mother. My father was very upset. He told my mom to be sure that this would not happen to any other of his daughters. Then I told my mom, something is not right. I have skin hanging. I showed her. So, she arranged with the missionary clinic doctor to fix it. He used anesthesia and cut the remaining hanging skin. I had no pain, and I felt better now. At least a little more normal.

Assala

My uncle, Ketema, wanted me to come live with him. I was the only child of his favorite sister, my birth mother, and I looked just like her. He loved me and vowed to take good care of me. So, after a couple of months, I accepted his invitation, joined him in the town of Assala and enrolled in school there.

One afternoon, I told him what Dureti's mother had done to me during my summer vacation with their family. When he heard this, he slammed his fist on the table and yelled, "She has ruined your life!" I was still too young to really grasp the meaning of what she had done. I still thought I was being a "good girl." My uncle said, "You will understand when you grow up." He just left it that way.

Living with my uncle in Assela was heaven. He was working at a Swedish company called Ardu. Housing for Ardu's workers was in a huge, gated compound with beautiful villas inside.

I was living in one of the villas with my uncle and his youngest brother. We all had our own bedrooms, and we had a live-in maid who cooked breakfast, lunch, and dinner. I was put in charge of managing the money for food and managing the household.

In the compound there was a clubhouse, supermarket, tennis court, basketball court, table tennis, etc. I could go to the supermarket and load up on anything I wanted, especially chocolate! The food was imported from all over the world.

In this luxurious lifestyle, I was beginning to metamorphize out of my tomboy days into a young woman. I started to dress up like the pictures I saw in fashion magazines. I took the pictures to the local seamstress and had her sew things up for me that were modern and stylish. I had a problem though…big feet! I could rarely find shoes in my size.

I had a best friend there called Melu. We were inseparable. Melu had a beautiful older sister who we wanted to match up with my uncle. So, we had a party in our house and invited her. She was pretty, smart, and had a great job. My uncle liked her, so they started dating.

There were three single guys living in the villa next door. One of them dated my friend Melu. He brought me chocolate, too. So, my uncle and Melu's sister, Melu and her boyfriend, and I, all five of us, were all having a great time together.

My uncle went on a business trip once or twice a month. So, I would stay in the house and go to school and stay with the maid. One day, our neighbor, one of the three guys living next door, invited me to dinner at his house. His name was Yetbark. He always flirted with me, but I thought it was a joke.

I told the maid where I was going. She warned me, "Be careful." When I arrived for dinner, I was greeted warmly. It was a big villa with five bedrooms, but, I discovered, no one else was home, not even the maid, and the house was deserted.

I walked in to find that his bedroom door was wide open with romantic music playing inside. The table for our candle-lit dinner was set up in the bedroom. I was really nervous. We ate dinner. Conversation was tense.

After dinner, Yetbark grabbed me and told me he had been looking forward to this day and thinking about me for a long time. He told me I was never alone and always surrounded by people like bodyguards, so he could never tell me his true feelings. He said, "Tonight is the night that will bind us together." He knew I was a virgin, and I knew it was his intention to take my virginity. My mind was racing. How could I escape this moment? I did not resist his hugs or kisses. After a very intense moment of physical contact, he became very aroused. He took off his clothes and jumped into bed naked. I told him, "Let me take a quick shower and freshen up. I haven't taken a shower all day." I put my shawl on the bed to make him believe I would be coming back. Then I grabbed a clean towel from his cupboard. I left the bedroom door partly open so he could hear the sound of the shower. I went to the bathroom and cranked the shower on. I left the towel on the floor and tiptoed to the living room towards the outside patio. Because the shower was running, he could not hear the latch on the big door.

Since we were next-door neighbors, I didn't have far to go to get back home. I ran to my house and banged loudly on the door. I called to the maid, "Open the door quickly." I was afraid he might be following me. She opened it and said, "Did he take your virginity?" I told her, "No." She told me, "Sit down in that chair." She had me spread my legs to see if I was bleeding; I wasn't, of course.

She said, "God love you. I knew he was up to something, that bastard. He waited until your uncle was not home to take advantage of you."

The next morning, I was still terrified. I told his friend Muhamed who was dating my girlfriend, what Yetbark had done. The only people who knew what had happened were the maid, Muhamed, and Melu. I kept it a secret from my uncle because I didn't know what he would do. He might have beaten him up or killed him.

A pattern emerged that plagued my young life. On one of those occasions, the wife of my uncle's friend, Dr. Jonny, was sick, so he asked me to help take care of their little daughter. I spent all day at their house babysitting. As evening approached, Dr. Jonny insisted that he give me a ride home in his car, even though we lived very close to each other. When we arrived at my house, he stopped the car and before I could get out, he grabbed me and tried to force a kiss on me. He hadn't counted on my boldness. I pushed his head back hard and scratched him. I just jumped out of the car and ran into the house. I was sickened and disgusted by this older man's behavior. I had just helped his sick wife and taken care of his child, and his response was to sexually attack me.

My youngest uncle opened the door for me. I ran past him, rushed to my bedroom, threw myself on the bed, and started sobbing. My young uncle came to my bedroom to see why I was crying, and I told him what Dr. Jonny had done. We decided not to tell big uncle because if I told him everything that happened, he might attack his friend and get in trouble himself. But I became especially wary of my uncle's friends.

After a year, my uncle's job was transferred to Debre Zeit. To say goodbye to our neighbors, we gave a huge farewell party at our villa. All my uncle's friends and their girlfriends and wives were there. I played hostess. We were serving an Ethiopian wine called Tej. It is made from fermented honey. Food and drink were flowing, and our guests had a great time.

After everyone left, on his way out the door to drive someone home, my uncle suggested that since I had never had alcohol, I should try the wine. Tej looks and tastes just like orange juice. The wine was delicious and sweet and went down easily, but I had no idea about controlling how much I drank. When my uncle came back, I went to open the door and hug him, and fell right out the door into the rosebush. My uncle had to carry me to the bedroom. I had passed out.

The next morning, I was covered with bruises and scratches. My uncle lectured me, in a nice way, to be careful with alcohol. He wanted me to have my first drinking experience in a safe place.

Uncle was helping me grow up safely. He even spoke with me about sexuality and how not to get pregnant and to value my body. He told me that when I finished high school, I could have a boyfriend and I wouldn't necessarily have to marry him. In traditional Ethiopian culture, if you have a boyfriend, you have to marry him. I trusted my uncle completely, and he counseled me through my early relationships with men. My dad and my uncle have been the biggest role models and mentors in my life. They taught me to have self-respect as a woman, and also to respect others.

Since I needed to continue with my schooling, and my uncle did not yet have a home in Debre Zeit, I went back to Kuyera, which is about 196 kilometers south of Addis Ababa, to study at the Seventh Day Adventist College. I joined my uncle later that year in Debre Zeit when he had a home for us.

Our home in Debre Zeit, was a beautiful place with four bedrooms, coffee plants, huge peaches, avocados, papaya, and beautiful roses in the front yard. And, again, we had a maid. As in Assela, my job was to run the household and handle the expenses.

My uncle was a very handsome single gentleman with a good job. And it seemed all the single women were attracted to him. To get next to him, women would give me presents and try to be my best friend. I enjoyed all the attention and the extra popularity!

There were always guests in our house, and we went to wonderful restaurants and bars. I was surrounded by well-educated people, doctors and engineers, all living the good life. My uncle took me to fancy parties in nearby mansions given by these "elite" men. I saw women, all dressed up, bussed in from Addis Ababa to be their "dates." I saw them publicly making out and going off into separate rooms by themselves. I was just objectively watching and learning like an anthropologist. I became determined not to be like those women who were just there, letting themselves be used. At one party, a man came up to me and complained that I was like my uncle's "wallet"—no one could get next to me. Thanks to my uncle, that was true.

I remained a target of my uncle's well-educated and accomplished friends. They were all men of power and privilege who felt they could sexually abuse a young girl and face no consequences. Whenever I was caught alone in the house, or one of them happened to be spending the night as Uncle's guest, or even if they happened to stop by the house, they would try to "get" me. Should I tell Uncle? If I told, would there be a divorce? What about their kids? What about my uncle having no friends left? In reality, if I had told, he might have shot them and then he would be in jail. I was torn apart, but I managed to defend myself against all of them.

Uncle Ketema with me at the reception in San Francisco

Much later in life, when my beloved Uncle Ketema was dying of a malignant brain tumor, I went to stay with him in California during his last days. I read this manuscript to him, and he listened carefully to the stories of what his "friends" had done to his little niece. He was shocked, amazed, and impressed that I had fended them off successfully.

Eyob

While I was in high school in Debre Zeit, I met a college boy, Eyob, through a mutual friend. I fell desperately in love! Eyob and I met once in a while in a secret place. In my culture, everything must be kept secret unless you are going to get married. There is no dating. I thought this would be the man I would spend the rest of my life with.

I could not concentrate in my classes, and my grades were dropping. He was at the university in Addis Ababa forty miles away, so I couldn't see him often. I teamed up with the maid and told her everything. She would carry love letters back and forth between us. When I would see him, my heart would start beating hard and my voice would shake. It was a true first love.

One day we got a chance to meet at the home of one of his friends. I had told my uncle that I was studying. This is the first secret I had ever kept from my uncle. I spent all day with Eyob. He told me he had gotten a scholarship to go to Washington, DC to study engineering. My heart dropped. He said he would wait for me, no matter what. "I'm not taking your virginity," he said. "Keep it until we see each other in the US." It was very clever of him, because as a virgin, I couldn't have relations with anyone else and would have to wait for him.

He finally got his visa to go to the US, and he left. I felt a knife in my heart and cried for a long time. I thought I would never find another man like him. His brother and I went to the same high school, and we saw each other every day. I stopped eating much, lost weight, and did poorly on my exams. My uncle noticed that I had withdrawn from social life. When I got Eyob's first letter with a picture enclosed, I read it in my room, crying, and put it under my pillow. We kept up communications for a year until I finished high school.

After high school, I was motivated to try to leave the country both because I longed to be with Eyob and I had always dreamed of exploring the world. My childhood friend, Dureti, was engaged to a man who worked for Ethiopian Air Lines. He had a best friend in Holland who visited him frequently.

He showed his friend a picture of me with my friend, Dureti. When he saw my picture, he insisted on meeting me. So, Dureti's fiancé introduced me to his friend in Holland by phone. We began to communicate and exchanged pictures and letters for about a year.

His name was Seid. He sent me an invitation to come to Holland to attend the Seventh Day Adventist College, as he was a member of that church. I had relatives who lived in Denmark who had met Seid and were in touch with him about my coming.

It seemed I would have a support system waiting for me in Holland, so I began my application for a visa. Because one of my late uncles had been Sport and Cultural Minister, it only took one phone call to the Dutch Embassy to obtain my visa.

During my communications with Seid, I had made it clear that I was not coming to marry him. I was coming to go to school and that we would have to get to know one another and then we would see if that led anywhere. I was not sure exactly what I would encounter, but I was bold and excited about my trip. It was 1984.

Seid

I was thrilled to be starting a new life in another country. Maybe it's because I grew up in a Swedish missionary school with white kids, or maybe it is just in my character. Unlike most Ethiopian girls, who were just looking forward to marriage and children, I always wanted to explore.

The plane took off. I could see my mom and dad waving goodbye. My dad was wearing a three-piece suit and my mom was wearing a traditional white Ethiopian dress with embroidery around the edges and a scarf over her hair.

I started to cry. There was an older man sitting next to me who comforted me. I was cradling a traditional Oromo porridge pot on my lap as tears streamed down my face. It was a very long trip.

Finally, I arrived in Berlin where I stayed in a hotel for the first time in my life. Everything was completely unfamiliar. I didn't know what to eat. There was a huge buffet with strange food. I just picked up some bread and jam. I was looking everywhere for sugar until I noticed someone open a paper packet and sprinkle sugar into their tea. Then I did the same. I had trouble sleeping in the big bed in the big hotel room all by myself.

The next day I had to wait all day in Berlin for my flight, which wasn't until the evening. It was an all-night flight. Exhausted, I arrived in Amsterdam.

When I came off the plane, Seid was standing there, waiting for me with flowers in his hands, but he was not smiling. He was short, light-skinned and basically a "nice looking" guy except for the cold look in his eyes. He took me directly to his house.

The first night I was very jet lagged and tired, and he left me alone. However, after a couple of days, he started showing me his "devil side." He roughly, cruelly, painfully raped me over and over again. When I tried to resist him, he told me I was totally under his control. He said, "Just get used to it." In between raping sessions, I would go to the bathroom, get down on my knees on the cold hard tile and pray to God to help me get away from this horrible man. I was in a strange country, did not know anyone and didn't know the language. I was completely at his mercy.

To survive, I knew I had to escape. He had no job and stayed home all day watching and controlling me. I could not eat. The rape continued.

One night, I had enough of it. I screamed at him, and he left me alone. While he was sleeping, I went into the kitchen and picked up a big knife. I walked into the bedroom. I was standing over him, frozen, with the knife raised ready to stab him, when a voice came over me that said "No! put down the knife."

I put the knife back, sat down on the couch shaken and shocked by my actions. I knew it was time to exit. My mind was racing as I looked for any opportunity to escape. I had a family member living in Denmark, but when she called me, I could not speak a word because Seid was always sitting next to me, listening. When I wrote a letter, he would read it. There was no safe way to communicate about my situation with anyone.

By now I had been imprisoned and abused by Seid in Amsterdam for two straight weeks. Unexpectedly, he told me that he knew an Ethiopian couple that he wanted to invite to his house. In his twisted mind, he thought we could do something "normal" together. I told him it was a great idea. They came. Mimi and Tadde were so sweet and kind. For the first time since my arrival, I had someone to talk to. Mimi and I seemed to understand one another immediately. While her husband and Seid were talking, she asked me if all was well. I shook my head, "no" to give her the message silently. She sneaked her phone number to me and told me to call her and she would show me around Amsterdam. Then they left.

After they left, Seid told me to tear her phone number up and warned me to never call her and never to tell her what he was doing to me. I instantly memorized her number and tore it up.

Things got worse. But now, at least I knew someone in Holland. After a few days, the couple invited us to their house. It was not far from where I was being held captive.

Seid warned me not to tell them anything. I promised him I would keep my mouth shut. I would have promised him anything. He decided it was safe for him to take me to their house. Here was a man who imprisoned and raped me while he was, at the same time, trying to act as if things were normal and we had some kind of relationship that could be shared with others. I played along.

We walked to their house. I memorized every step, every street name. When we got there, we were warmly welcomed.

Mimi left Seid and Tadde with snacks in the living room and told them we were going into the kitchen to cook. I could see Seid's eyes follow me and darken as I walked into the kitchen without him. I didn't care. Once we were in the kitchen, I hugged Mimi and broke down. She comforted me and calmed me, and I poured my heart out to her, telling her everything Seid had done to me since arriving in Amsterdam. She herself began crying, and we leaned on each other's shoulders, hugging and sharing our raw emotions. She promised to get me out of this situation and away from Seid.

Then, we started to cook. After we finished cooking, we went into the living room to serve the food. I could see the fury bubbling over in Seid. He began speaking to me in Oromo so they wouldn't understand. He asked me, "Why did it take so long for you to prepare this food? What did you tell her in the kitchen?" He knew that I had told her. He could see that my eyes were red from crying.

I had told Mimi in the kitchen that I did not want to go back with him. She said, "No, you have to go back. We are going to use a strategy to get you away from him." So, we just ate dinner, thanked them and left their house. I was so happy. It felt like I had found my own family. Meeting Mimi and Tadde made me feel that they would help me get out of this mess. Finally, there was hope.

We walked home in silence. Once we arrived home, he cornered me and demanded to know what I had told her. He was screaming in my face. I said, "I didn't tell her anything. I just talked about Ethiopia." He and I both knew I was lying, of course.

The next morning, I told him, "You cannot force me to have sex with you. You cannot treat me like this. Be kind and gentle and treat me with respect. I am not going to be here forever!" He slapped my face so hard that I saw stars. I answered his slap, "You cannot keep abusing me forever. Kill me, I don't care!" He was taken aback by my boldness and actually apologized. Strangely, he said, "Sorry, I will never do it again."

One Saturday morning he decided to take me to the Seventh Day Adventist Church. I was surprised because he had never asked me to go out with him other than to Mimi and Tadde's house that one time. They had kept calling to check on me, however.

It was a rainy day, and I was not feeling well. I refused to go to church and so he let me stay home. I asked him for a guilder to buy bread at the supermarket and he gave it to me. I was really surprised. Then he said, "I'll see you later." I watched him go, peeking out the window. He came back and asked me to give him my passport. I said, "Here you go," gave it to him and he left. I made sure he got on the tram and was really gone. For the first time, I was completely alone in the house. After that, I never looked back. I walked out of the house with only an umbrella and a little notebook with family member's phone numbers. I left everything there and walked, following the directions I had memorized. I was concentrating so hard that I was nearly hit by a car. I remembered every step.

I arrived at their house and rang the bell. I yelled, in a panic, "Open the door quickly!" I thought he might be following me. Her house was old and had a lot of stairs, so it took her a long while to get to the door. Once she came down and opened the door, I was so relieved. When we saw each other, we both began crying. I told her I would rather die than go back to Seid's house.

Mimi said that she and her husband would help me to start my own new life. I felt that I had been reunited with my own family. She let me have a warm bath and gave me some dry clothes. We sat on the couch drinking tea, waiting for Tadde to come home. I told her all the ugly details of Seid's abuse.

We were still huddling together and drinking our tea when Tadde walked in. He was shocked to see me. Tadde hadn't really known the details of what I was enduring until Mimi explained it to him in this moment. He said, "I knew something was wrong. I am going to report him to the police." Mimi told Tadde, "Calm down. Let's find a peaceful solution." While we were discussing everything, the doorbell rang. Mimi went downstairs to open the door. There was Seid, standing there, asking for me. She told him, "Yes, she is here," and invited him to come inside. When he came inside, the first thing he said, in Oromo, was, "What are you doing here?" I answered in Amharic, a language that Mimi and Tadde understood, "I am not going back to you after everything you have done to me. I want to contact my family in Denmark." He replied in Oromo. "You don't know them. They are going to sell you. They are gay and they are going to use you." I translated what Seid was saying. Tadde got very angry and jumped up and said, "Get out of my house!" Seid stood up and told me to think about it and call him and left.

I felt so free. I felt that nothing worse would happen to me than had already happened. We had a home-cooked Ethiopian meal together, and I rested.

I called Koonie, my family member in Denmark. Her phone number was in my little notebook I had taken from Seid's house. Koonie was overwhelmed by the story of my kidnapping and rape by Seid. She took the first flight she could and was there the next day. Since she knew Seid, she went to his house to get my passport. He returned the passport on one condition. "Get her out of this country. If she stays here, I will destroy her or kill her. If she is not going to be with me, she won't be with anyone. I will destroy her life." Koonie was in shock. But she assured him that she would take me with her back to Denmark, so he gave her my passport.

I stayed with Mimi and Tadde for a while. They were so sweet, protective, and nurturing. They had me sleep between them, in the middle of their big bed. I was having so many nightmares, waking up screaming in the night, that they wanted to stay close to comfort and calm me.

Word spread through the Ethiopian community in Holland about what had happened to me. A lot of generous people raised money to take care of me and get me back on my feet. Tadde took me to the doctor. Thank God, I wasn't pregnant.

Nijmegen

Sadly, I couldn't get a visa to go to Denmark. So, it was decided to send me to Nijmegen, far away from the capital, to arrange for asylum. Nijmegen is the oldest city in Holland with grand historic buildings and plazas on the Wall River.

It was a beautiful exile. I rented a little room with a folding bed and stove. Here, I was free of bondage but far away from my family and I was living alone for the first time in my life.

My landlady, Yaneke, enrolled me at Erasmus University to study Dutch. I met people from all over the world there. And, finally, I began to feel more content. My social worker, Marsha, was working on my application for asylum. In less than a year, I was granted asylum. Marsha familiarized me with all the shops and sights in town and gradually, I became independent. I also had a great tutor, Peter, a kind young man who really helped me with my Dutch. He taught me a phrase and told me to say to my landlord, "*Ik heb een schattig kontje.*" I later learned that I was saying, "I have a cute butt." Peter laughed every time I said it. My landlord told me those were bad words and not to repeat it.

One day Peter invited me to his parent's house for dinner so he could introduce me. I was so welcomed by his parents and felt very special. They cooked a delicious meal. I made a comment about the meat being the most delicious since I had come to Holland. The mother replied, "Yes, we only cook this for our special guests." It was horse meat. "What?" I said. I went into the bathroom and put my finger down my throat and tried to vomit, but I couldn't. I was disgusted at having eaten a horse, one of my favorite animals in the world.

I found a Lutheran church and started to attend regularly. I met a wonderful Dutch family there. Every Sunday, after church, they took me to their house for dinner. I looked forward to church and spending this wonderful time with this family. They became my surrogate family.

On Christmas, there were presents under their tree with my name on them. They gave me a bicycle, the main form of transportation in Holland!

One afternoon, now that I had transportation, I decided to go to the zoo by myself. I was walking around in the zoo, and I met this guy named Winnie. He asked me if I was from Africa. He asked my name and told me that his wife was also from Africa, so I immediately felt comfortable with him. We walked around the zoo, and I gave him all my contact information. I was so naïve. Here I was, having given all my information to Winnie, trusting him because of his African wife. Just a couple of days later. I heard the doorbell ring. I went downstairs to open the door. And there was Winnie. I asked him, "Where is your wife?" He replied that she was working that day and told me, "I just stopped by to say, hi." In my culture, if someone shows up at your door, you have to invite them in. I invited him in for a cup of tea even though I felt uncomfortable at that point. I offered him some tea and started a conversation. While I was making tea, he laid down on my bed with his arms and legs open. When I returned with his tea, I was shocked and said, "What are you doing?" He got up and drank his tea. I made up a story that I had to meet a friend at a certain time so he would have to leave. He left. I asked him to bring his wife next time. I knew on some level that something was up. After a couple of days, he called and wanted to see me again. I told him I was busy with exams. He kept calling. I thought, "Hmm, this married guy keeps calling me. What's this all about?" I didn't know what to do, so I called my good friend from Somalia, Wilka. I told him what was happening with this guy who kept calling me. Wilka was like my brother and protector. Finally, I told Winnie to meet me at a coffee shop and I brought Wilka with me. When we arrived at the coffee shop, I introduced him to Wilka and told him he was like my brother. Wilka told Winnie, "Don't you ever bother her by calling her or showing up at her door again." He said, "Let's go, Lily," shook Winnie's hand, and we walked out. Winnie never called me again. Later on, Wilka found out that Winnie is a well-known pimp! In Holland, there is a lot of open legal prostitution. People from all over Europe go to Holland for legal drugs and sex.

After living for a couple of years in Nijmegen, Holland, I planned on moving to Utrecht to study tourism. Just before I made the move to Utrecht, I was invited by a friend to Amsterdam to participate in a reception at a travel agency. It was about an hour train ride. I arrived at the Amsterdam train station, then had to take a bus to get to the reception. As I was walking towards the bus, I saw Seid for the first time since I had left him. He was walking toward me. My whole body got numb when I saw him. I kept walking toward my bus stop. When I arrived at the bus stop, my bus was already there. When I looked back, I could see that Seid was still following me. I told the bus driver, "My life is in danger." Then Seid got on the bus. "He is following me to harm me." The driver told me, "Sit next to me. When you get off if he is following you, I'll call the police." Then Seid said in Oromo, "Are you Telile? You are still here? You didn't leave? Hmmm." He just sat there as the bus pulled out onto the street. It was quiet. When I arrived at my destination, the bus driver said to me, "Step out, I'll wait for you." He stopped the bus.

I exited the bus. When I looked back, Seid was following me. I tried to get back on the bus, but he ran up to me and pushed me and grabbed me by the arm with his left hand. With his right hand, he reached into his pocket. I held his right hand tight and screamed. The bus driver got out of the bus and a woman was hitting Seid with a shoe. Other passengers attacked him as well. Then, when I released his hand, he dropped a 6" switch blade on the ground and ran for his life. In the meantime, the bus driver was calling the police. The police arrived. They took me in for questioning. I told them, "If anything happens to me in this country, it will be Seid who is responsible. He has threatened my life and the lives of my friends." They took testimony from all the witnesses. Then, they said they could not arrest him because he had not yet done anything to me. But they would keep this information about him in their records. The police gave me a ride to the reception. My friends had been worried about me because I was so late arriving. Now, I knew that Seid was serious when he said, "If I can't have you, no one can have you!" I spent the night in a hotel with a couple of friends. The next morning, I took the train back to Nijmegen.

Now, I was living in fear and was hyper-alert wherever I went. I thought he might be able to find out where I was living. I heard through Ethiopian rumors that he had a picture of me and was going around asking people to help him find me.

Right after the knife incident, I moved, as planned, to study for work in the travel industry. Things calmed down. I responded to a newspaper advertisement for a roommate and met two girls, Alice and Marijo. I moved into a room in a big house with a lovely garden. We agreed we would pool our money, they would do the shopping and cooking, and I would do the dishes. They were vegetarian, so I became a vegetarian too. I went to school full-time and on the weekends; we rode our bikes, cleaned house, and had wonderful meals together.

It was my birthday month, June 1989. Prior to getting a job with an airline, I worked in a restaurant to make some quick cash. I met the owner, Omar, through one of my friends, Huda. For my birthday, Huda and Omar planned a big party. They invited all my friends. It was a surprise party, so I was told that Huda's parents were having me to dinner, and I should come to their house directly from Amsterdam to Den Haag train station and bring an overnight bag.

After I met Huda and her boyfriend at the station and got in the car, I realized that we were not traveling towards her parents' house. She told me she had to pick up something from the store, but we went to Omar's restaurant. When I entered the cocktail bar, it was filled with everyone I knew in Holland. They had copied my address book. Mimi and Tadde, the people who had rescued me from Seid, were even there. I felt a mixture of frightening memories and the love I felt from all these wonderful people.

I was hungry and thirsty and there was a birthday cake, so I had a really big piece. After a little while, I began to feel sick. A huge sense of panic overtook me. I felt that my pounding heart was going to jump out of my chest. I thought I was dying. I pulled my friend, Ada, into the bathroom. I told her how I was feeling. My body was on fire, and I started screaming for help. People rushed in to help. I was thrashing around on the floor so hard that four men couldn't hold me down. They carried me to the emergency room at the hospital where the doctors thought I was just being hysterical. They gave me sleeping pills, and Ada took me to her house where I slept for 24 hours straight. Periodically, she shook me awake to get me to eat something.

I talked to people who had attended the party later and learned that a lot of them had been feeling strange after eating the cake. My girlfriend's boyfriend had even had trouble driving. The owner of the place, Omar, had baked a hashish cake and drugged everyone at the party. I wrote him a letter telling him that I never wanted to see his face again.

Mustefa

Around 1988, I went to an elegant event with my friend, Ada. There, I met a very handsome man named Mustefa who was visiting from Turkey. We exchanged phone numbers and became good long-distance friends. There was a year of casual friendship before I agreed to date him. He invited me to Turkey a couple of times, and we toured the sites together. He was always charming and respectful, and I always had my own amazing hotel room. I did not question at the time why he never took me to his house. He would frequently come to visit me and take me out whenever he came to Holland on business. But I began to wonder about his status. I would learn a year later, after a life-threatening trauma unfolded, what his intentions were.

December 11, 1989

I was working for temp agencies doing odd jobs while I attended tourism training at I.T.A. (International Travel Association). I studied to get my diploma so I could work in a travel agency. After receiving my diploma, I started looking for a job. A good friend of mine, who had a big travel agency, got me a job at Bangladesh Airlines. I began commuting from Utrecht to Amsterdam on the train five days a week.

All my friends had warned me not to work in Amsterdam, but I felt that I could not let fear of Seid rule my life, that I had to keep living my life, regardless. The concept that this man would actually hunt me down and kill me was hard to keep alive in my consciousness as I developed a successful new life in Holland. I was in denial.

Sometimes I would stay late after work with friends and take a late train home. Until Dec. 11, 1989.

I left home in the morning to go to work as usual. It was such a busy day that I decided to take a late lunch. I had a date planned for that night as well. It was a really cold winter, so I was dressed in a heavy coat, gloves, and boots. I decided that once I finished my work, I would have lunch and run some errands.

I was walking down a busy, crowded street at around three in the afternoon when I looked straight ahead and there was Seid, coming toward me. He looked really run down. His clothes were disheveled, his hair was all messy. His eyes were wide and wild as he stared straight at me. We passed. I kept my head high and kept walking. Suddenly, he was right next to me, grabbing my arm. "You are still here, huh?" he said softly. I pushed him away and ran towards a big jewelry store, but the store was closed. I kept running and went to another store. He got close to me and grabbed me again. I dropped the bag I was carrying, shoved him again, and ran. There was a huge white pillar that I hid behind as I ran. There was an open store across the street. Now, I could not see where he was as I ran towards the store.

I heard shots zinging past my ears, Psss, Psss, Psss. He had a silencer on his gun. There were five shots. When I entered the store, I told a woman, "Please call the police and an ambulance." She began to scream and cry. She said, "Let me take you upstairs." I felt the blood streaming down my right arm and soaking through my clothes. She dragged me upstairs, and I collapsed on the floor. I felt dizzy and nauseated. The ambulance and police came immediately.

They started cutting off my clothes to see where I got shot. I was moving in and out of consciousness, but I was able to answer every question that the police asked me. "Who shot you? Did anyone else know him?" I even told them about the 1987 police report when Seid had tried to attack me with a knife. I gave the officer Tadde and Mimi's phone number. I was holding the police officer's leg tight for support and my blood was getting all over him; I apologized. He said, "Your life is more important than my trousers." It warmed my heart, and I smiled at him.

I began gasping for breath and gagging on blood. They found that I had been shot in the hand and I heard them say: "*he wordt in de maag geschoten,*" which I knew meant I had been shot in the stomach. When I heard that, I started to panic. They wrapped me up and carried me downstairs to the ambulance. I still couldn't breathe. They gave me oxygen. I could hear the sound of the siren ringing in my ears as they sped me to the hospital.

When we arrived, they carried me in on a stretcher. There were five doctors all suited up in their surgical greens waiting for me. They went up in the elevator with me and took me directly into surgery. The bright lights were blinding. There, I met Dr. Paul. He was asking me questions, "*Spreek je Nederlands?*" "Do you speak Dutch?" I said, "Ja natuurlijk." "Yes, of course." I asked him in Dutch, "Do you think I will survive?" He said, "Yes, let's pray and let's begin." While he was talking, I slipped into the painless sleep of anesthesia.

When they opened me up in surgery, they discovered that a bullet had passed between two ribs without touching them and from there through my liver, lodging within one centimeter of my heart. It was a miracle. My abdomen was full of blood that they had to wash out to see where to do the repairs.

Out of five shots, three of which I heard zinging past my head, one had passed through my arm and the one that had lodged near my heart was safely removed. It was a miracle.

When I woke up from my surgery, I was in intensive care. The first person I saw next to me was Ada. She was my emergency contact. I looked up at her and yelled, "Run, run, run for your life!" I couldn't stop my tears. I cried buckets of tears while in the hospital. I was alone with no family and in a foreign country, but I did not tell my family about this attempted murder. They couldn't come, and I didn't want to worry them.

I was heavily medicated, so my mind was not clear. I was frightened by the many tubes and machines attached to me. They hadn't sewn up the hole in my arm, it was just draining. There were stitches from my navel to my sternum. Dr. Paul came to check on me every day. He told me, "I have done a lot of surgeries. And your survival is a miracle." He pinched my cheek gently and said, "God has a plan for you, kiddo!"

By the fourth day, I was out of intensive care. I was in stable condition, but I was unable to eat. I had bled so much that the doctor said I needed a blood transfusion. I begged him not to give me a transfusion since I had no family to donate blood. He agreed to try medication for a couple of days. I began eating a bit. I had a hard time keeping the medication down, but I was so determined to make it work that I just kept taking it. After a week, I had another blood count. The doctor said, "I have good news for you. You no longer need a blood transfusion." My blood count was okay. However, I was still feeling very short of breath. The doctor ordered an x-ray, and they discovered fluid in my lungs. They gave me medication, which helped, and my breathing improved.

The police came to me for questioning as soon as I was in stable condition. I told them who shot me. I told them that he had tried to kill me with a knife and that there was a police report. I could not let my guard down though, because the guy who shot me was still on the loose.

After the police interviewed me, they were able to find Seid. He was in his house watching TV. They searched his house. The gun was not there. However, the instructions for the gun were there, which matched the gun that was used on me. And there were witnesses. He was arrested.

People were streaming in to see me. It was overwhelming. There were flowers everywhere. The Ethiopian community was all lined up to comfort me. They only allowed six people at a time to come in. My Dutch friends were there as well. It was so incredible how loving, kind, and sympathetic people were towards me. Some were in tears of empathy.

I stayed in the hospital for two weeks, getting better every day. After they removed the stitches, I began to walk a little, holding a pillow tight against my stomach to stabilize my guts against the pain. I had a hard time looking at my scar while they removed the stitches. I was a young woman, and I was now scarred for life.

There was no comfortable position in which to sleep. Eventually, I was able to extend my walks in the halls. I talked to lots of people during the day. At night, I was afraid to sleep because of the nightmares, so I hung around the night nurse's station. The hospital food was horrible. I wasn't eating and was losing weight rapidly. So, my friends divided up the days and brought me home-cooked meals every day. I began to regain weight.

The time came for me to be released from the hospital, but I was terrified of going back to my apartment alone. We drove to my apartment, grabbed some clothes and drove straight to my friend Zed's house. She gave me her only bed in her one-bedroom apartment. I started physical therapy close to her house every day. My social worker took care of all the arrangements. I had a psychologist who was helping me walk through my fear and my grief. The fear was really bad. Any sound would make me jump. I kept hearing the sound of the silenced bullets passing my head. And sleep was still next to impossible.

During the time I was staying with Zed, my Turkish friend, Mustefa, came for a visit. He was shocked at how I looked. I was very thin and frail. We had a short visit, and he returned to Turkey. We kept in touch.

Slowly, I began to recover. Eventually, I was able to move back to my apartment. Zed came to stay with me while I got used to living in my apartment again.

I had to appear in court to testify against Seid. My group of friends and my social worker all came to support me.

Seid was there with his court-appointed lawyer. He was alone except for maybe one guy. All the chairs in the courtroom were filled with my supporters. I was trembling when the judge asked him, "Did you shoot Telile?" He answered, "No, maybe it was someone who looked like me. All blacks look alike." The judge said, "There are ten witnesses. The bullet matches the gun type in your manual, and we have the police report of an attempted stabbing in 1987. So, you are telling me that you didn't do it?" Seid said, "No." The judge decided that since he had no prior record, he would give him a six-year sentence. So, that's all he got. I was angry that he didn't get more time. I was relieved, though, that he would be behind bars for six years and I wouldn't have to worry about him for that time.

I finally called my family and told them what Seid had done and everything that had happened and assured them that I was now fine. I decided to go visit them in Addis Ababa. I spoke with my social worker and my therapist, and they supported the idea. I hadn't seen my family for several years. I bought my ticket and had a much-needed healing time with my loving family.

Mustefa's Intentions

On my return to Holland from my visit with my family in Addis Ababa, Mustefa contacted me and invited me to have a vacation in Turkey. I went to meet him in Istanbul. When we were face to face, having dinner, I confronted him. "Why haven't you ever had me to your house?" He told me that when he was young, his family had an arranged marriage for him. However, he was free to do whatever he wanted. I was very upset. "Why didn't you tell me that in the beginning?" I asked. He said, "It's not a big deal." It was a big deal to me. I never would have gone out with a married man. Then, he said he had been married for 16 years and had no children. He asked, "Would you be willing to have a child for me?" He said he would take care of me for the rest of my life and I could live on any continent in luxury. The idea of having a child and not being married shocked me. I came from a culture where first, you would get married and then have children. He kept trying to convince me it would be fine, and I should do it. I was still reeling with shame about him being married and him wanted me to have his child. I told him, "No way would I ever do this. No amount of money will change my mind. When I get pregnant, it will be with a loving man who will be there to hold my hand through the pregnancy and the birth of our child." I would not settle for less. After a long discussion, he understood there was no hope for his idea. I returned to Holland after this visit, cut off our intimate relations, and we never talked about it again. However, he became a lifelong friend who would always be there for me and when he did find a woman to bear his children, they were born into my hands.

America

After I returned to Holland, my friends were telling me it was time to leave the country for my own safety because eventually Seid would be out of jail. I decided to go to America and visit a friend for a couple of months and see how I liked it. I bought my ticket and traveled to Los Angeles. I told Mustefa about this experiment and he said he would financially support whatever I needed for this journey.

When I first landed on US soil, I had been invited by my dear friend, Nina, who went to high school with me in Ethiopia. We had both lived in Europe. She lived in Italy while I was in Holland, and we had kept in touch. In Italy, she was in an abusive marriage to a guy who was half Ethiopian and half Italian. He beat her so badly that she had a miscarriage. She had family in Washington, DC who were trying to get her into the US. Eventually she made it and was living with a guy in Topanga Canyon in LA when she invited me to come for a visit.

I arrived in LA in 1990 and made it quickly through customs. I stood in front of the airport looking for Nina. I was tired, nervous, and jet lagged and she wasn't there! She has been known not to respect time! Finally, after about an hour, she arrived. She used "traffic'" as her excuse. I soon learned that in LA, that's a real thing.

So, here I was with my old friend, Nina, driving to Topanga Canyon in a Jaguar with the top down. It was wonderful. I was in heaven. America the beautiful. The weather was warm. She was living in a big house with a couple of dogs. When we arrived, there was a big gate and a long driveway to her house, which looked like a palace to me. She helped me with my luggage and took me to the room where I would be staying for a couple of weeks. After I freshened up, her husband came home, and she introduced me. I almost fell off my chair. He was way too old for her! She was young and beautiful, and she settled for him? He took us to a wonderful dinner in Malibu. We got back home, and I went straight to bed.

I woke up early and still could not fathom why she was with him. She came to my room, and I started asking, "Why, why him?" She told me that he was very nice to her and helped her when she was in need. She had met him while working in a restaurant as a cocktail waitress. He assured her that if she went out with him, he would take care of her for the rest of her life. Basically, he bought her. He was nice to me and treated me with respect during my visit. And, gradually, I began to understand their relationship because he was so kind, and Nina had been so abused by her first husband. Now she felt safe and happy with this older gentleman.

They took me to Las Vegas and various places so I could see more of America. Then, Nina introduced me to Gerta. Gerta and I became instant friends. She was from Haiti. Her dream had always been to travel to Europe. So, I invited her to visit me in Holland.

Gerta introduced me to her husband, Arnold. They decided that while I was in the US, I should really see it. We took a road trip on Highway One along the coast of California. I saw Santa Barbara, Big Sur, and Carmel. We drove all the way to St. Helena in the wine country. When we stopped for lunch in Sausalito, a beautiful hillside village overlooking the bay across the Golden Gate Bridge from San Francisco, I told Gerta and Arnold, "If I ever move to the US, this is where I will live."

The day for my return to Holland arrived, and Gerta and Nina dropped me at the airport and waved goodbye.

I arrived safely back in Holland and got back to my life there. Gerta arrived soon after, and we toured Europe together. We got along really well and had a great time couch surfing through Europe on the cheap, staying with friends. I kept in contact with Gerta and Nina after Gerta's visit. But I stayed in Holland only one more year.

I now knew I had to leave Holland. I was worried that since he had only been sentenced to six years, when the crazy guy who tried to kill me got out of prison, he would try again. I was no longer under any delusion or denial of what he was capable of.

Before leaving Holland, I invited all my friends to my apartment and told them to take whatever they wanted. We had a great party with a lot of laughter and tears, and I said goodbye to everyone and my life in Holland. It felt like I was leaving a part of myself behind. All I had were two suitcases and one carry-on bag to start my new life in America. But I was going to the land of freedom.

Leaving Holland

When I landed in the US, Gerta was right on time and picked me up at the airport. She and her husband gave me a room in their house where I could stay until I found a job and a place of my own. Gerta was incredible! She helped me get my driver's license, which is absolutely essential in Southern California. After looking at ads for jobs in the paper, I settled on looking for a babysitting job. I responded to an ad from Malibu. Gerta lent me her car. I arrived at the huge gate of a mansion. I wanted to live there! They opened the gate, and the family was waiting for me in the living room. There were two kids, husband, and wife.

When I walked in the door, the kids were instantly connected to me and I to them. Then, the mother said, "Have you ever tried modeling? You are beautiful." I told her that I had done some modeling but wanted to improve my English. And that I loved children. The father and the kids wanted to hire me. But the woman, not so much. She told me that I should go and pursue a modeling career instead. That happened over and over again.

I answered another ad in Sherman Oaks. He opened the door and said, "Lily, come on in." He shut the door. My heart began beating hard. I was very ill at ease with this guy. He told me that his wife had died, and I would be traveling a lot with him and his kids; he asked me if that was okay. It seemed that he was looking for a lot more than a babysitter. He said, "You've got the job. When can you start?" I assured him I was interested in the job and would call him. And I got out of there. He kept calling. I kept not answering. After several more unsuccessful interviews for a babysitting job, I realized that it was not going to happen, and I closed that door.

Eventually, while in Los Angeles, I went to school and worked two jobs to support myself. I sold shoes at Nordstrom, was a restaurant hostess, and a student. At that time, I was living with my California boyfriend, David.

When I was in the middle of taking my final exams in fashion merchandising, I got a letter from my father telling me, "I am going to jail. Please take care of your mother and brothers and sisters." That was such a shock that it threw me into a panic. I was terribly frightened for my father's safety.

To help, David's grandmother sent an invitation to my father to visit her in the US. With that invitation, he was able to get a visa and come to LA. He left Ethiopia on a Friday, and the men came to arrest him the following Monday. He stayed a couple of months with us in LA. It was very uncomfortable for me because David and I weren't married. In the beginning, I didn't know what to say to my father. However, he seemed to understand, and he liked David a lot. But he said that I should marry him. My dad was very grateful to be alive.

Since we had family in Portland, Oregon, we decided that would be a better place for my dad to live. He would have family nearby. Eventually, he was given political asylum in the US. I moved to Portland to be close to him and David followed me.

I worked at Nordstrom and helped take care of my dad. I became the number one person in sales there. But I was miserable in Portland. I hated the rain and the cold. And I began to question my relationship with David. I didn't want to marry him. So, I decided to end it.

My uncle Ketema came to Portland from Ethiopia on sabbatical leave from his work as a veterinarian. I decided to put my uncle and dad together so they would have each other, and my uncle moved in with my dad.

I had a vivid dream about my friend, Rob. My friend, Dureti, (who was cut with me) was living in Portland, too. I happened to run into her, and she said, "Oh my God, he was just asking about you." Dureti gave me Rob's contact information in the San Francisco Bay Area, and I called him. Rob encouraged me to transfer to the San Francisco Nordstrom store.

I told David, "I am not happy in the relationship, and I am leaving." I decided to move to Palo Alto and work at Nordstrom there. I rented a U-Haul truck, loaded my stuff into the truck and towed my car behind. My uncle

Ketema drove the truck to Palo Alto for me. It was the first time he had driven the freeways of America. It was so stressful that he got sick.

Finally, we arrived in San Jose. I put all my stuff in storage, and we went to a motel in Palo Alto. It was the cheapest tiny motel there. The toilet was right in the bedroom. We had to take turns leaving the room so the other could use the bathroom. I had my car, but I had to wake up very early in the morning to move it because of street cleaning. I was already working at Nordstrom. I asked my uncle to stay at least one week before leaving me alone.

While I was working at Nordstrom, I was asking people where I might find a roommate. I had to get out of that motel. One Sunday, I said to my uncle, "Let's go to church." I flipped opened the yellow pages. I said, "Whatever church comes up is the church we will go to." So, my finger landed on the Menlo Park Baptist Church.

I parked my car, and there was a woman sitting outside, smiling. She said, "Welcome." She invited us to sit with her in the pews. After church, we exchanged phone numbers. So, Monday morning, my uncle flew back to Portland, and I moved in to briefly stay with my new church friend, Monica, in San Mateo.

I was still working at Nordstrom, when another new church friend, Linda, invited me to her house for Thanksgiving. I was so excited to go. At that time, Linda was newly divorced. She was living in one bedroom of a huge house in Woodside. She invited me to live with her. Even though I did not know her that well, I felt an instant connection. I moved in.

We had so much fun going out together. I was meeting new people. Life was good. I lived there about a year. Linda's mother, Lois, and I really clicked. Again, I had a new family.

On this six- acre property, there were two cottages that they rented out and the main house. One cottage became vacant. I asked Lois, Linda's mother, if I could rent the cottage below market rate. She said, "Let me think about it." The next day she said, "I can't think of anyone who deserves to live in that cottage other than you." So, I got all my things out of storage and moved in. It was heaven! I had just bought a new Volkswagen Beetle. Linda and I enjoyed her six horses in the stable. I learned country western line-dancing. I even got some Tony Lama boots! We were like sisters.

My uncle did not like living in Portland, so I invited him to come live with me in my little cottage in Woodside.

One night, during the weekend, I went to a party at a big house in Woodside. It was only five minutes away from my cottage. As I was driving home, I had to cross a little bridge. There was a car coming toward me with bright lights. I realized when it got close that it was going to hit me head on. I veered off the road and hit a big tree. The air bag deployed. My right hand was shattered, my left collarbone was fractured. My lip was split open. The woman who nearly hit me with her car came and physically pulled me out of the car. She asked me where I lived. She put me in her car. I thought she was taking me to Stanford Hospital, but she was just taking me to her home. I was in agony with my broken hand just hanging there. She left me in the cottage alone with her 14-year-old son. I was screaming for help.

She took my uncle back to the scene of the accident to drive my car home. It was not drivable. When my uncle and this woman arrived at the scene, the police were already there. The police were asking questions of both of them.

The police came to the cottage to get me. They took me back to the scene to do a sobriety test. When I blew into the tube to test my blood alcohol level, it tested above the legal limit because of the blood in my mouth. They asked me to walk in the dark. When I stumbled, they handcuffed me, even though my hand was shattered, and I was telling them that I was in agony. Clearly my arm was broken, and my hand was just hanging there.

They escorted the woman to the gate of her home and took me to the police station in Redwood City. I told them that I had Stanford Hospital Insurance, and it was the closest. After hours of crying in pain, they finally took me to the County Hospital in San Mateo. I was admitted to the hospital and finally my injuries were addressed. First, they sewed up my lip. I had to wait for the orthopedic surgeon to arrive to do surgery on my hand. They put in six screws and sewed me up. When I was released, my life was upside down. I had a cast from my right shoulder to my fingertips and a sling on my left arm. My lip was sewn up, and I had bruises everywhere. I was basically immobilized.

The police charged me with DUI. I had a lot of friends helping to take care of me. One of my friends got donations to hire a well-known DUI lawyer. There were two trials. The best thing was that a friend insisted on taking a picture of my injuries for evidence. The DUI trial lasted one day. The lady who caused the accident was testifying under oath. When her 14-year-old son was questioned, he told the jury his mother had been drinking all day. The police never questioned her about her sobriety but just escorted her home. I won the case and the charges against me were dropped.

Then, the DUI lawyer found a civil rights attorney who sued the police and the woman for racial profiling and discrimination. We had expert witnesses. It was a one-week trial in federal civil court. I won that case, too. The police only got a few weeks' paid leave. It was liberating to have won this case against police discrimination and brutality. I was glad I had spoken up against it. This was my first experience of racism.

During my recovery, I could not work and was on disability. People I did not expect to help me came to my rescue. The chef from the local restaurant came to cook food for me in my kitchen. Someone put $4,000 in an envelope. Another restaurant delivered food once a day. So, my refrigerator was full.

It seemed that I knew everyone in town, and they all stepped up to help me. I had my hair done for free by the local hairdresser. My house was cleaned, my clothes were washed. I couldn't even brush my teeth or wipe my bottom for three months. Linda did that.

While I was recovering, ironically, I broke my foot while just walking on the street. A bone density test said my bones were normal. So now, I had a boot on one foot as well.

I took that time, while I was completely helpless, to think and to realize that I had, once again, survived a brush with death. I felt humble and grateful to be able to heal my wounds and live. But the reality of my helplessness was wearing on me. One day, I was sitting on the couch, crippled and broken, with tears rolling down my face. I made a decision. I wiped my face of tears with my one good hand and decided to move on with my life in a positive way. In the back of my mind, I felt my life had been spared for a reason. I just did not know what it was yet.

Following this accident and the long recovery was a time of experimentation with how and where to live my life. I had tried a series of relationships (serial monogamy) years long, with some very nice men. I had worked in fashion, found financial success, and was completely dissatisfied with all of it. I left the jobs, and I left the men.

Standing on the floor at work at Nordstrom, I heard myself talking out loud, "I've got to get out of here. This is not my life. I've got to do more than this!" I was the number one salesperson, and I was miserable! I had enough and gave my notice that day with no idea of what I would do next to support myself.

After I got home, I was in a panic. I called my friend Billy in San Diego and told him I had just quit my job and didn't know what to do. He said, "Great! My company will pay you while you get your real estate license. You will be great at it." I jumped on the idea and was really excited.

I got my license and began working as a mortgage broker. Sitting in an office cubicle looking at those walls closing in on me felt like being in prison. Again, I heard myself saying, "This is not my life!" I had to tell Billy I could not continue in real estate. This was a time when brokers were giving variable rate mortgages to people who, later when the rates went up, would lose their homes. I could not in good conscience participate in that.

While still working in real estate, I met Tom through a mutual friend. He was looking for a house. Tom was my client. But, somehow, we always seemed to have appointments near the end of the day, and he would take me to dinner. He found a house he liked, but still, we would have dinner together. This expanded to going for hikes and eventually to a trip to Sea Ranch on the coast. After about a year of this, I was thinking to myself, "This is a really nice guy." He was kind, generous and funny. Then we started dating in earnest.

After a few of months of dating, I became pregnant. I never thought I would get pregnant, but here it was. Tom and I decided to get married, and we set the date, May 28, 2006. Although I had some reservations, in my culture, a pregnancy outside of marriage would be a huge disappointment for my family, especially for my father. I just wanted to do the right thing.

The wedding was huge with a beautiful cake in chocolate and vanilla to represent us. My family was in heaven because I was finally married. I was the oldest of seven children and they were afraid that I would end up alone. They all loved Tom.

I stayed in my apartment until we could find a place where we could live together. I had to go to the doctor for a check-up. My gynecologist told me she had some sad news. I had an ectopic pregnancy. The embryo was attached outside my womb. She told me I would have a miscarriage. I said, "It's okay, it was not meant to be." She was so sad I felt the need to comfort her, but I was numb.

A couple of days later, I started cramping. The cramping was so painful I was rolling around on the bed. Then it was over. It felt like this little life had been ripped out of my body. Sadness washed over me.

After that, I would go on long walks to the beach where my cell phone would not work so nobody could reach me, and I could just stare out at the ocean. I tried to distract myself with decorating our new house, but the sadness was always there.

I decided to find out why I had lost this child and if I would have children in the future. So, I went to a fertility specialist who examined me. He told me that my ovaries were like those of a young girl, but I was not producing eggs normally and to become pregnant, I would need fertility treatments. This is such a personal decision. For me, I feel so strongly about accepting my natural fate, the body that God gave me, that I could never agree to such a process. I put the possibility of having children out of my mind.

Life went on. Since I didn't have to work to support myself for the first time in my adult life, I had a window of time where I could reflect. Tom and I traveled. I dabbled in small ventures. But an uneasy feeling of emptiness began to grow in me.

I knew that, after surviving all the close brushes with death, and after losing a potential child, I was still alive for a reason. I concluded that I needed to search for a purpose for my life. I began to read books about spiritual fulfillment and inspirational biographies. I asked myself while I hiked the hills and valleys of Marin County, "Why am I here? What is my purpose?" It became a mantra, filling my head in the rhythm of my footsteps. During this time, I felt myself withdrawing from my marriage. I was completely preoccupied, traveling to visit my family and basically living like a single woman. That, of course, put a strain on my marriage.

Finding My Purpose

In October 2008, I emailed family and friends and told them I had decided to return to my birth village of Kofele to search for my purpose in life. I was having such vivid memories of my childhood there that I knew that was where I should go. I was just listening to my inner voice and following where it led me. My friends and family donated $5,000 for me to do some good in Kofele. I was overwhelmed at the support and felt validated to follow my heart.

So, after 25 years away, I returned to my birth town, Kofele, Ethiopia. With $5,000 in my pocket and love in my heart, I traveled home. I knew Ethiopia had changed since I had left as a girl. But I wasn't prepared for the magnitude of the changes that I saw. The poverty was heart-wrenching and the plight of the children, especially of the young girls, was truly saddening. I cried a lot. Seeing our fellow human beings in this condition, our hearts must open.

Life has not been the same since this visit. Tears were frequent and I could not shake the sadness that I felt from what I saw. At the same time, the joy I felt in giving to these people during my visit reset my values and goals in life.

I knew I couldn't help everyone, so I decided to help one family in a way that would immediately better their lives. I learned that one of my birth mother's brothers was very poor. He was living with eight children, in a mud hut with no kitchen and no bathroom. In one week, I was able to have a house built for them. It had two bedrooms, a kitchen, and a bathroom. I had a little money left over after building the house and was looking for another way to help.

My brother-in-law had been feeding homeless people through his church. He took me to this ramshackle assortment of blue tarps and cardboard boxes fastened together with tattered rope next to a cemetery. We managed to feed over two hundred people in one day. I was thinking, these people living next to the cemetery are so close to death. There was a blind person. There was a woman who had just delivered a baby. People were young and old. All of them were hungry. We gave them a traditional Ethiopian meal and drink. They were blessing us, and we felt blessed in return.

During the construction of my birth mother's brother's home, I met Ubo. At seven years old, Ubo worked as though she were an adult, cooking and cleaning. One day I decided to have a little chat with her. I took her photograph and when I showed her the picture, she told me, "I didn't know I was so beautiful." She had never seen her own image. Her name, in our native language of Oromo means "beautiful." I choked back my tears.

Ubo

That was the day I made the decision to do all I could to make sure no girl would grow up without knowing how beautiful she was or having the opportunity to go to school.

And especially, no girl would be a victim of gender-based violence, genital mutilation or being forced into marriage at an early age destined to premature childbirth and illiteracy. I bought Ubo school uniforms, school supplies and left enough money to supplement her nutrition.

After returning home, I was so exhilarated by seeing the change of the family in the home I had built for them, I thought at the time I would just raise $5,000/year and build a home for one family at a time. However, the plight of the young girls was so dire that my focus shifted. I remembered girls and women carrying wood and water. The image of sick, hungry little girls, some of them pregnant, some of them carrying babies, with no hope for their future haunted me. I realized I had found my purpose.

Upon my return from Ethiopia, my marriage was still not going well. So, we ended the marriage, and I moved to Sausalito with just the clothes on my back. I got a small apartment and started all over again. While I worked towards developing a new organization, I also worked as a hostess at a restaurant, and as a caretaker of a woman who had been injured in a bicycle accident. Tom and I remain good friends. And he became one of the earliest and most loyal supporters of my mission to help young girls.

The next time I went back to Ethiopia, in 2010, I was determined to help more girls. The process of recruiting girls took place in a Swedish missionary compound. There was a gate with a guard. It was a very sunny day. I was hopeful that I might be able to find sponsors for 20 girls at $1/day. When I arrived at the meeting place, there was a very long line of girls waiting. They were all hungry looking, with distended stomachs from parasites, and in rags. These were the poorest of the poor.

I sat at a small table and wrote the name of each girl on a piece of paper. We pinned the paper on the little girls' shirts and took their pictures. The line was so long and the girls so needy that I had a very hard time saying no to anyone. And so, the 20 girls I had planned to help became 51 because, at the end, there was one set of twins. Their mother came to me and said, "You separated my twins." So, I took them both. Finally, with people begging me to take more girls, I had to ask the guard to shut the gate. With tears in my eyes, I knew I had to stop. I had no idea how I would get sponsors for 51 girls, but I said a little prayer and took all their pictures home with me.

When I returned to Sausalito, a local friend and I took the pictures of the girls and showed them to everyone we could think of. I was excited and unstoppable. I took a binder with pictures of the girls to coffee shops and spoke to strangers. I convinced them that for the price of their coffee, they could sponsor a girl and change her life. When a girl was sponsored, I put a happy face sticker on her picture. I was fired up and happy. People in town were saying, "Oh, oh, here she comes." Through the compassion and generosity of many people, within a few months, we were able to find sponsors for all 51 girls. I wired the money to buy them school uniforms, school supplies, health care and nutrition. And they were all treated for the water-born parasites that infected them due to a lack of clean water.

The following year I returned to find them miraculously transformed from sick, lice-infested, starving girls with lifeless eyes into bright, healthy schoolgirls. The girls lined up before me to give me a hug. My heart could not contain my joy. Before, I had cried for their hopelessness. Now I cried tears of joy.

On my return to the US, with the encouragement of friends and family, I founded a 501(c)3 non-profit organization, Tangible Hope Foundation, so that people can make tax-deductible donations to support the health, education, and protection of young girls.

Because these little girls are still vulnerable to kidnapping and rape, we obtained land in Kofele where we have begun to build a safety/educational enrichment compound. It is called Adu Darara, which means Sun Seed in Oromo. The building will be a sanctuary where they can study and grow into womanhood in safety. Here, they will become empowered girls, able to teach others how they can grow into women who can change their own world.

I still cry when I return to Ethiopia, but now I cry tears of joy at how well the girls are doing. I now know that it is my purpose in life to help more and more girls learn to help themselves to a future full of hope and opportunity. They, in turn, will lift future generations out of the cycle of poverty, ignorance and violence.

Health Issues

While working on my mission for the girls in the US, I found out that my mother was rapidly losing weight. The doctors did not diagnose her cancer for six months. By that time, her lung cancer had spread to her spine, ovaries, and liver. It was hopeless. We couldn't understand how this could have happened. My mother never smoked or drank and lived a healthy lifestyle.

My mother had been away from Ethiopia for eleven years and wanted to go back to see the two daughters she had left behind. She was given two rounds of chemotherapy and was then able to travel home one last time to say goodbye.

Upon her return from Ethiopia, her health deteriorated quickly. I was traveling back and forth between Sausalito and Portland, Oregon to visit her. While I was visiting with my mom, I felt a burning pain in my right side that would not go away. I came back and went to my doctor and told him my symptoms. I knew something was wrong and insisted on having an ultrasound. On a Friday afternoon, my doctor called me. He said, "I have bad news. There is a fifty percent chance that you have a cancerous cyst behind your kidney. I made an appointment for you on Monday to see a kidney specialist." I didn't want to believe him as I was consumed with grieving for my mother. And now, again, I had to be concerned with my own life as well.

On Monday, I went to see the doctor. He pulled up the MRI on a computer screen and told me the cyst behind my kidney was growing and had to come out right away. I said, "Give me some time. I want another opinion." I went back to see my mom who was not doing too badly at that time. The doctor referred me to a kidney transplant specialist who gave me the same opinion. He said, "Have the surgery right now!" I made an appointment for the surgery. I was communicating with my mom who said, "Don't postpone your surgery. Just do it." I had a consultation with the surgeon and begged him to do laparoscopic surgery because I have so much scar tissue in my body from all my injuries. He said he would do his best. I had the surgery, and it was a malignant cyst. However, the miracle is that my body had encapsulated it thoroughly. They took part of my kidney to be sure they got it all.

I was on the phone with my mom every day. She hid from me the fact that she was going downhill rapidly. My sister called me at the hospital to report on my mom's actual condition.

I was released from the hospital after one week and I was determined to see my mom. My doctor told me I could not fly. I broke all the doctor's rules, bought my ticket and flew to my mother's side to be with her before she died. She opened her eyes and asked, "Why did you come? You just had surgery." I told her I was fine. That was it. She never opened her eyes again. Mom passed two days after I arrived. Hospice had given my family a book about what to expect when my mother was dying. It was a step-by-step description. We put flowers in the room and played soft classical music. I sat by my mom, taking my pain medication every two hours.

Witnessing my mother's death before me and feeling completely helpless, I could do nothing but watch over her with my two brothers and my sister. There was a coldness that began in her feet and traveled up her body.

Her death was peaceful. When she took her last breath, we didn't want to call anyone. We just closed the door and sat there with her for several hours. Finally, we called, and they took her body. She wanted to be buried in Ethiopia, but we had a service in Portland first and the attendance was amazing. So many people loved her. My brother and I were asked to read her eulogy. I did, even though I was still holding my side in pain. Later, her body was flown back to Ethiopia. I visit her grave every time I go there. Even though I had escaped death so many times myself, what I saw gave me a real understanding of how peaceful death could be and my fear of it has subsided.

The Path to Success

While I had dedicated myself to helping the girls, I had somehow neglected to make my own welfare a part of my plans. I worked three jobs so that I would have the flexibility to be able to work towards Tangible Hope's mission. I would have daytime meetings with potential helpers/donors and then work as a hostess in an Italian restaurant in the evening. I managed property for people who kept a house in Sausalito and only visited occasionally.

The hardest job was as a caretaker for a 56-year-old woman who had become paralyzed in a bicycle accident. In the beginning, I did not want to take this job, but her plight haunted me. I had empathy for her, and we became very close. I knew that if things had turned out differently, with all the violence that I had endured, I could have been in her shoes.

Taking care of her involved very intimate jobs, changing her catheter, shaving her legs, cutting her toenails, etc. I worked very hard to inspire her to walk again. I stayed with her for over a year. By that time, she could get on her feet and walk a little. Working three jobs became emotionally draining and physically exhausting. But it was what I had to do to maintain Tangible Hope and take care of the girls.

I was working those three jobs when I met Janet. I had been invited to speak at the Sausalito Woman's Club and she was sitting in the audience. As I spoke, there were tears rolling down her cheeks. She had worked with children with disabilities, written grants and was retired. I had a small raffle that day with Ethiopian spices and an Ethiopian scarf in a basket. She won. She offered to help that day and has been with me ever since.

Janet is patient. When I become frustrated with the inevitable setbacks that come from trying to change the world, and say, "I am done!" She calms me down. Janet says, "We will go over, under, around and through any obstacles that get in our way. We will just keep moving forward, walking our path in the direction we must go to help the girls."

Janet helps me with correspondence. I tell her what I want to say, and she will write something and read it to me. I say, "Janet, you get me." And, Janet says, "That's what I do. I 'get' Lily and communicate her vision to the world." Working together creatively has been a joy for us both. We "know" each other on a deep level. We laugh often. We speak words we are thinking at the same time. We are doing a "dance" together while we are working to lift up girls in the world. It is exhilarating. It is magical. It is a blessing for us both. I cannot forget Janet's husband, Floyd, who has been so helpful, supportive, and generous with Janet's time.

A really upsetting and disappointing development was the sudden unexpected dropping of the girls by some of their sponsors. I really took it personally. I couldn't sleep. What could I tell them? Were they going to have to stop going to school? They were dropped by people who could well afford it. I could barely support myself, so I couldn't take up the slack. I felt sick to my stomach. I asked myself, "Why am I doing this? Why am I going through this grief?" Then I looked at pictures of the amazing transformation of the girls and my faith was restored. I had to keep going.

This unexpected shock came right before I was having a fund-raising event. A sponsor who was (through her company and along with some of her contacts) sponsoring 25 girls informed me that she and they were no longer going to support them. I was shocked and horrified. I had to scramble to find new sponsors for them all. Janet set up a table with the binder and their pictures at our fundraiser. I had to tear off the happy face stickers of the girls who were dropped. We got them all new sponsors. And now, they are all still in school, thank God.

In 2012, there was a contest on the website of A Band of Women to get free tickets to attend a lecture by a woman's rights advocate. I entered the contest and won a ticket. It was a catered event at a private home. I walked in alone, standing tall, wanting to meet people with a mutual interest in the rights of women and girls. I walked into the kitchen. There was a man sitting in a chair at the kitchen counter. He rose, walked up to me, shook my hand and said, "How do you do?" He asked my name. He asked me what had brought me to the event.

I was fresh from Ethiopia and so excited, having just returned from seeing the amazing change in the girls. I was anxious to share the story. I told him everything about what I was doing. He listened. And he asked me for my card. People were standing behind me waiting to talk with him. He said, "I have a dear friend who might help you."

There was a woman who followed me to the patio. She asked me, "Why is he so fascinated with you?" I answered, "Well, I was just telling him about the foundation I started." She said, "Do you know who he is?" I said, "No." She said, "He is Peter Coyote. Do you know who that is?" I said, "No."

That is how Peter became a true friend and an advocate for Tangible Hope. He wrote a recommendation to the Rex Foundation, (Jerry Garcia's Foundation) and we got our first grant, $5,000. That was a big deal. I had to stand on the stage of the Fillmore Auditorium in San Francisco in front of about 700 people with musician Mickey Hart and a band standing behind me and give a speech.

I spoke about the impact of this grant traveling from San Francisco all the way to Ethiopia. Then the band began to play, and the scent of marijuana drifted across the room. While I was sitting in the Fillmore Auditorium with Janet, a woman came up to us and introduced herself. Her name was Vickisa. She looked at me and said, "You are the real deal! I would like to interview you on my Point Reyes radio show." We made an appointment, and I did my first radio interview. I learned that Vickisa is an artist in Bolinas, California, and have enjoyed her friendship and support ever since.

Near the end of 2013, I went to pick up Tangible Hope's mail at the post office and there was a letter. It was from an organization called Wisdom in Action. There was a Buddha on the envelope. I almost threw it away because I thought it was junk mail. When I opened it, it said, "You have been selected to receive the 2014 Unsung Heroes of Compassion Award from the Dalai Lama. Do you accept this invitation? If so, please sign and RSVP." I looked at the letter. Then, I looked around the car and back to the letter. I called Janet and read it to her on the phone. Then, I brought it to her house, and we read it together to see if it was real. Janet said, "We have to RSVP right away."

The journey to the February 2014 Dalai Lama event was filled with planning. There was a professional writer assigned to write my biography. At that time, I wasn't ready to talk about all the early traumas in my life, but I did tell her I had several brushes with death, which motivated me to find a purpose for my life.

The event was amazing. There were 52 individuals from 18 different countries. They all came together at the Ritz Carlton Hotel in San Francisco. The first day, we all gathered together in a circle in a big white tent. These people, who came from all over the world, were all doing something wonderful for humanity.

I met Miguel who had lost his own child. He was helping over 700 street children in Peru. There was a woman from South Africa who was working for a white man under apartheid. Her parents had died. He took her to the doctor and had her fallopian tubes tied so he could use her for sex without her becoming pregnant. She did not learn that she had been sterilized until later, when she and her husband tried to have a child. She was receiving the recognition from the Dalai Lama for her work establishing the Amazing Grace Children's Home as a safe place to feed and house poor street children. There were two men, a Palestinian and an Israeli, who were hugging each other and working for peace. There were so many inspiring stories. They are all in a book published by Wisdom in Action for the 2014 Unsung Heroes of Compassion event.

What I will always remember was the spiritual feeling of oneness, of being there together for one purpose—compassion—in the same space, at the same time. I am humbled to have been in the presence of these people and will never forget the palpable, positive spiritual energy filling that tent and permeating the following day with the culmination of the personal presentation of the awards by His Holiness the Dalai Lama.

Epilogue

Again, life is uncertain. I had been planning to go to Ethiopia in September 2019 and this time, I was going to bring my father with me. After 25 years in exile in the US, he felt, under the new leadership of Prime Minister Dr. Abiy Ahmed, it was now safe to return home. He also felt returning home would be good for his health since he had been diagnosed with cancer and was starting to feel weak. He said Ethiopian air is better, and he would be rejuvenated in his home country.

I planned to stay in Ethiopia for two months. So, to save money, I moved out of my apartment, gave away most of my belongings and put the rest in storage. I stayed with dear generous friends until my departure.

Everything was going to plan when my dad's health suddenly got worse, and I had to go back to Portland. The doctor told my sister that our father only had a few months to live, but she didn't tell me until after I arrived in Portland. I stayed to take care of him, and he deteriorated quickly. It was my father's wish to be buried in Ethiopia. So, I made a quick trip back to Sausalito to retrieve my passport.

I rushed back to Portland on July 24th and dad passed away peacefully at home on July 25, 2019. My sister and I were by his side. We made the necessary arrangements to ship his body back to Ethiopia and my brother and I flew there on August 4, 2019.

I had forgotten the traditional mourning rituals of the Ethiopian culture. It brought me back to the death of my birth mother to hear the screaming and wailing of all the people who came to give their respect to my father. They surrounded the house. There was no quiet, peaceful time to grieve.

It was a four-hour trip from Addis Ababa to carry my father's body to his resting place in Kofele. The procession was three miles long. Three thousand people attended his memorial. He was a much-loved governor and peacemaker. My father was buried next to my second mother and his siblings in the land he loved.

Having lost the two most important men in my life, my father and Uncle Katema, I began to work out how I would move on without them. My father and Uncle Katema had supported and blessed my work to educate and empower young girls. I could hear their voices in my head urging me on. I used the energy of my grief to throw myself into my work.

I was able to arrange a meeting with the president of Ethiopia, a woman named Sahle-Work Sewde. She was very gracious and agreed to support my work on behalf of young girls. There was a lot of media attention, and I was energized by her support to renew my efforts.

Then, the COVID global pandemic hit. I felt it was safer to isolate myself away from the crowded capital, Addis Ababa. So, I traveled to Langano, a resort area on a lake where I stayed in the vacation home of an old friend. My brother and cousin joined me. Because of COVID, there were no tourists. It was a quiet time of reflection all over the world as people stopped their busy lives and reevaluated what was most important to them. I was doing the same.

While we were resting and enjoying the lake, someone approached me and asked if I was interested in buying a little shack on the lake. With the financial help and encouragement from friends and family, I took this golden opportunity. I began to design and build a house on this large plot of land with beautiful lake views. It was to be built with the stones that were already there.

This would be a compound with cottages where donors could stay. They could explore the richness of Ethiopian culture, visit the place where human beings took their first steps, and enjoy the incredible birds and other wildlife of Ethiopia while visiting the girls they support.

It was a challenge to build on my land as a woman hiring a male contractor. I have a wonderful, talented cousin who came to my rescue to help with the building project. When he sees my creative ideas, he only laughs and enjoys the process of building together. I am forever grateful to him! Now, the compound is nearly finished, and beautiful landscaping and trees are being planted. It will be a welcoming place for the donors of Tangible Hope to visit!

It is with great joy that I share with you that Tangible Hope has our first college graduate! She was recruited into our program as a poor, hungry little waif at the age of seven. Now, she is a beautiful, healthy, happy college graduate.

From my grandmother, Ako, through my birth mother, my father, my auntie/mother and my Uncle Ketema there has been a golden thread of love sewn through the fabric of our lives. And now, I pass that thread on to my 140 daughters of Tangible Hope.

Tilile (Lily) Yoseph
Founder/CEO
Tangible Hope Foundation

About The Author

Author Telile (Lily) Yoseph was honored to be chosen to receive the Unsung Heroes of Compassion Award from the Dalai Lama. In addition, she was a Pathways to Peace delegate to the United Nations Commission on the Status of Women in March of 2019 where Lily was among 9,000 enlightened women from all over the world who are rising up against all forms of gender discrimination. Each participant, in her own way, is creating a new pathway for future generations of girls to walk into a brighter world of opportunity.

This story is not meant to be a story just about gender inequality in Ethiopia, but a global story of women who are waking up and demanding their rightful place as equals alongside men bringing the balance that female voices can bring to all societies.

Lily was born in Ethiopia. Although she was raised in a loving middle-class family, the fact that Ethiopia is one of the 20 poorest countries in the world with a long history of human rights abuses makes her birth country, along with its culture, a contributing character in her story.

As you have read, Lily has personally experienced some of the worst human rights abuses imaginable and was nearly killed on multiple occasions. "God has not only made me a survivor," she writes. "He has given me the strength and courage to fight back against sexual predators, two of whom have served jail time for their acts of violence against me and other women."

This is Lily's first attempt at revealing her personal story of survival, strength, and inspiration. She believes these God-given gifts not only enabled her to overcome unspeakable attacks but inspired her to create a non-profit foundation to educate and empower young girls during their formative years when they are most vulnerable.

Tangible Hope Foundation gives young Ethiopian girls the knowledge and skills they need to not only protect themselves from sexual predators, but to obtain the education they need to lift themselves and their future families out of the cycle of illiteracy and poverty.

Today, Tangible Hope Foundation is making a difference in the lives of Ethiopian girls. Lily's vision, however, is not confined to Ethiopia, it is global. Woman and girls all over the world are learning that they do not have to become victims of sexual violence or abuse any more than they have to let themselves become victims of the poverty that surrounds them. Together, they are rising.

Acknowledgements

Most of all I wish to thank my loving family. Thank you, dad, for always believing in me and giving me the freedom to follow my dreams wherever they might lead. You taught me how to stand for the truth no matter the circumstances. You ingrained an unusual power in me with your example of love, bravery and truth-seeking.

My dad and Uncle Ketema with me in San Francisco on a beautiful afternoon.

Thank you to my birth mother who, along with life, gave me that all important unconditional love in my first five years that made it possible for me to stand tall and be independent. Thank you to my second mother/auntie who sacrificed her own path in life to be my new mother when my birth mother died. I often wonder how she would have lived had she not been forced to marry my dad. Her life was taken too soon. I wish I could give her one more hug.

Thank you to my uncle who raised me through those tumultuous teenage years. You taught me how to enjoy every day of life and not be constrained by traditional expectations of Ethiopian girls. You gave me permission to grow up and try my wings even as you were protecting me. You taught me not to worry about what others might think. You shared your beautiful homes and lifestyle with me and taught me to how to navigate socially in all walks of life. Though you are gone uncle, I know that your spirit will be with me forever.

There is a hole in my heart where my father, uncle and two mothers dwelt. Now that they are all gone, I still feel their guiding spirits carrying me through life until we meet again.

It is my dream that, as long as I live in this difficult, male dominated world I will share my story and encourage women everywhere to do the same. I have committed my life to help as many girls as I can to fulfill their dreams. And finally, I thank God for saving me to do this work.

"Life should not only be about living,
but also about giving."
—Telile (Lily) Yoseph

Printed in the USA
CPSIA information can be obtained
at www.ICGtesting.com
JSHW021952111023
50060JS00003B/9

9 798989 262403